30 DAYS
of HOPE

FOR RESTORATION IN INFANT LOSS

GIFTS OF HOPE SERIES

◆

THE "GIFTS OF HOPE" SERIES is a collection of 30-day short devotionals focused on various life issues and needs. Offering personalized Scripture selections and prayers that provide readers with inspiration and hope, these messages make wonderful gifts for the people in your life who need encouragement.

Forthcoming topics in the "Gifts of Hope" series include:

- ◆ Adoption
- ◆ Child Sickness
- ◆ Chronic Illness
- ◆ Financial Struggle
- ◆ Hurting Marriages
- ◆ Infertility
- ◆ Singleness
- ◆ Weariness

To learn more visit NewHopePublishers.com.

GIFTS OF HOPE SERIES

30 DAYS *of* HOPE

FOR RESTORATION IN INFANT LOSS

MAEGAN H. ROPER

NEW HOPE®
PUBLISHERS
Gospel-Centered. Missions-Driven.
Birmingham, Alabama

New Hope® Publishers
PO Box 12065
Birmingham, AL 35202-2065
NewHopePublishers.com

New Hope Publishers is a division of WMU®.

Library of Congress Control Number: 2015940130

ISBN-10: 1-59669-438-6
ISBN-13: 978-1-59669-438-5

N154116 • 0715

DEDICATION

TO MY BEAUTIFUL CHILDREN,
Emmalyn, Ellanie, and Harrison. Each of you is
a miracle of grace. It's such an honor to be your
mommy, and I love you more than words could
ever express. And to my loving husband and best
friend, Jeremy: I wouldn't trade any of our journey
for anything. Thank you for being you!

TABLE OF CONTENTS

• • •

• • •

My Savior, My King—I'll never stop saying thank You. You are greater than any grief experienced and Your love is always better.

••••••••••••• ᎒ᎯᏕ •••••••••••••

AND THANK YOU TO MY NEW HOPE FAMILY. IT'S A JOY TO DO life and ministry every day with this publishing team! To editors Melissa Hall and Joyce Dinkins—you've understood the gravity of this message and its importance to my heart, and you've kept it sacred. I've learned so much from your wisdom and ability to communicate truth. I couldn't imagine this content resting with anyone else.

Introduction

"It's a girl!" Those exciting words should be followed by conversations of pink, cupcakes, and lace. In our case, they were followed by a hard conversation with medical staff to learn that our daughter had a rare neural tube defect called *anencephaly*. Within minutes of learning we were having another baby girl, our world was simultaneously turned upside down, and we were changed . . . forever. I'm guessing that you've picked up this devotion because you're experiencing the same pain—the heartache of infant loss. It has many faces, many forms, but none greater in heartache than the other. They're all a loss, and they all change us. Though our daughter, Ellanie Beth, didn't survive her birth, her impact on our lives has survived and has touched many others' lives as well.

It's been said that there is no footprint so small it does not leave an impact on this world, and I know that to be true. I never knew what it meant before our loss to give birth to your heart and not be able to protect it. It has been a journey of sacrifice, pain, and joy. Joy, you ask? How can joy come from the loss of a child? My joy has come from gaining a new perspective of Christ's love for us and His sovereignty in our lives. Had I known then what I know now, I would tell myself, as I was sitting scared, shocked, and numb in that hospital room after learning our daughter's body was incompatible with life, that I would never know true joy, love, and grace like I would soon experience through this. I would tell myself that the Lord was preparing a harvest to come, and while it may seem like a drought now, plentiful rain would soon fall. Dear one, my prayer has been, since learning the Lord would allow this devotional to become a reality, that you would know this unspeakable joy and find it in your grief.

I know this is hard—to daily acknowledge the depths of your pain and face the realities of it. I do not want to discount that. This is by no means a ten-step process. This is a lifelong journey. A very hard journey that Christ wants to walk with you step by step, hand in hand.

In these 30 days, you'll find some bold statements, authenticity, a lot of Scripture and practical biblical truths, and advice for friends and loved ones, grandparents, and even dads. In praying for the Lord to craft this study to be as practical yet as biblically sound as possible, I prayed for you too—the reader. I understand what you're facing day in and day out, and I'm so ready to tell you that there is hope on the other side of this heartbreak. You may feel like a victim of the worst kind of pain now, but I assure you there is a Victor who rises above all burdens. Trust Him, cling to Him, and believe that your baby is waiting for you to worship with him or her in paradise. Forever is waiting . . .

Day 1

One Step at a Time

"I would have lost heart, unless I had believed that I would see the goodness of the Lord in the land of the living. Wait on the Lord; be of good courage, and He shall strengthen your heart; wait, I say, on the Lord!"

—Psalm 27:13–14 NKJV

· · · · ·

· · · · ·

Y OU CAN REJOICE IN THE RELIEF OF KNOWING THAT you are fully understood by the Lord. Others will not understand what you're going through. They'll try, and while they mean well, most of what they say will only frustrate you. And that's OK. God gets your struggles. Your feelings of inadequacy. Your hurt. And your hesitancy to move forward with a "normal" life.

I vividly remember having a come-apart in my parent's living room one week after we lost our daughter. It was December, and it just didn't feel like Christmastime. We hadn't participated in any of the usual traditions and festivities, and I hadn't bought a single gift. Not. One. It suddenly seemed to all come crashing down on me, and I

God gets your struggles.

found myself loathing "normal." I didn't want to get out and go shopping. I didn't want to attend Christmas parties or send out Christmas cards. What is usually so exciting and anticipated seemed unnecessary and daunting. And it wasn't, really. It was just my perspective at the time. And instead of approaching this grieving process one day at a time, as it slowly merged with my once normal life, I felt that I was supposed to shut off what had just happened and dive back into normal life.

That's not what God expects of you at all. The reality is that you'll have a new normal from here on out. It's almost as if your life becomes divided—before loss and after loss. And after loss, you do your best to get back to what you were doing before loss, but it just isn't the same and that's OK.

He has promised that we will see His goodness in the land of the living and give us courage to approach our new normal if we wait on Him. I think for the longest time I feared taking any steps into a new normal because I felt I was leaving my baby girl behind. When others would say "you'll move on", it didn't feel right. I know our natural human reaction is to leave a bad situation in the past, but part of me wanted to keep it in front of me as I moved forward, as a reminder of God's grace and the promise of future glory. There is no rulebook for the pace at which you should move. Don't rush, but don't be afraid either.

Those steps forward do not mean you love less. They do not mean you stop grieving or missing. They do not mean you forget. They do not mean letting go. Moving forward is about learning, growing, and trusting. You just learn to live in a world that keeps turning, even though yours stopped for a bit. Moving forward means turning toward hope and believing God is greater than it all.

· · · · · · · · · ● · · · · · · · · ·

Lord,

Help me to take the next step in You with confidence. Help me to move forward into healing knowing that You are with me. When the responsibilities of this world seem overwhelming in my grief and pain, surround me with Your presence. As I strive to take one step at a time, give me grace to trust that You long for me to live joyfully again. Open my eyes and my heart to experience that joy.

Amen.

Day 2
Toss Your Timetable

"He has made everything beautiful in its time.
Also, he has put eternity into man's heart,
yet so that he cannot find out what God has
done from the beginning to the end."

——Ecclesiastes 3:11 ESV

·　·　·　·　·

E CCLESIASTES 3:1–8 HAD ALWAYS BEEN FAMILIAR TO ME, I suppose because of its poetic nature. "A time to mourn, a time to dance, a time to weep, a time to laugh, a time to build up, a time to tear down"—it's a beautiful expression of a time and a season for everything. However, I had never read beyond those verses until our loss. Look at what follows:

What gain has the worker from his toil? I have seen the business that God has given to the children of man to be busy with. He has made everything beautiful in its time. Also, he has put eternity into man's heart, yet so that he cannot find out what God has done from the beginning to the end. I perceived that there is nothing better for them than to be joyful and to do good as long as they live; also that everyone should eat and drink and take pleasure in all his toil—this is God's gift to man. I perceived that whatever God does endures forever; nothing can be added to it, nor anything taken from it. God has done it, so that people fear before him. That which is, already has been; that which is to be, already has been; and God seeks what has been driven away. —Ecclesiastes 3:9–15 ESV

The Lord taught me, through studying this Scripture further in context, that we are so strained by our concept of time. It is very hard for us to wrap our feeble minds around the fact that God is outside of time. He has ordained things so that what was, is, and what is to come has already been set in motion by Him. Initially, reading this chapter of Ecclesiastes in its context brought peace and discomfort all at once. What's the uncomfortable part? That He is completely in control, even when I feel my life has gone terribly wrong and my dreams are broken.

When I tell my five-year-old daughter "no," she most often asks, "Why?" Lately, we've had numerous conversations that go somewhat like this: "Emmalyn, Mommy and Daddy know what's best for you. So when we say 'no,' you are not to question it but to trust that we have a good reason and move on." Does she like that answer? Absolutely not. Is she always compliant? Certainly not. But, she is learning, and little by little, day by day, the questions dissipate and her trust increases.

It is the same way with us as adults in relation to God isn't it? In our loss we may interpret that as God saying "no" to a child and we may be quick to ask "why?" because like little children ourselves, we don't always know what's best for us and cannot see the ripple effects that proceed into the future.

God, who is outside of time, knows exactly what He is doing. He has carefully orchestrated everything, both the good and the bad, both the joyous and the painful, to bring Him glory (Romans 8:28–31).

So, in your season of grief and loss, will you throw away your timetable? Do not be influenced by the voices of the world that may be telling you where you should be at this stage in your journey through loss. There are seasons allotted for times such as this. They are appointed by God to increase your dependence upon Him and strip away everything that hinders you from seeking the kingdom of God first. In the end, all wounds will be healed, all tears wiped away. Like Ecclesiastes said, "He has made everything beautiful in its time." He is making and will one day finish making all things beautiful, but until then, rest. And toss your timetable.

Lord,

Please help me to let go of my definition of time. I trust that you have carefully orchestrated everything in my life, even this difficult season I'm in now. Rather than follow how the world says I should grieve, help me submit to Your will and to discover what it is You want me to learn about You in this journey. Thank you, Lord, for the promise that You will never leave or forsake me! Thank You that Your yoke is easy and Your burden, light.

Amen.

DAY 3
ACKNOWLEDGE YOUR EMOTIONS

"Be alert and of sober mind. Your enemy the devil prowls around like a roaring lion looking for someone to devour. Resist him, standing firm in the faith, because you know that the family of believers throughout the world is undergoing the same kind of sufferings."

—1 Peter 5:8–9 NIV

· · · · ·

INFANT LOSS IS A UNIQUE EXPERIENCE. PARENTS HAVE intense reactions, not all of them acknowledged or addressed. Most parents' infant loss is private and unresolved. I'm sometimes shocked when hearing from older women of a different generation, who have encouragement to offer from their experiences of loss, that they never told anyone or dealt with their emotions. When we went through bereavement counseling, our counselor suggested several articles from the National Library of Medicine on statistics of grief patterns after perinatal loss. I think she was simply trying to help us feel normal in our emotional reactions, but I remember being stunned at some of what I read.

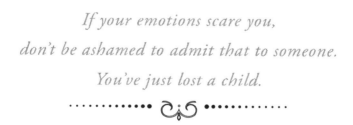

If your emotions scare you,
don't be ashamed to admit that to someone.
You've just lost a child.

I also discovered some statistics on parents experiencing infant loss in *Safe in the Arms of God*: 60 percent of parents feel angry; 50 percent of fathers feel guilt while 90 percent of mothers feel guilt; and 95 to 100 percent felt deep sadness.

I personally wondered if the statistics relating to guilt and anger were because those parents weren't acknowledging their emotions in public. Perhaps they weren't talking to a counselor or receiving any outward encouragement. Can I urge you to talk to someone or acknowledge—in some outward way—the sadness you're experiencing? Please don't be too proud to talk to someone about what you're going through. There are infant loss support groups at nearly every women and children's hospital. There are also several online communities I would recommend such as Share (nationalshare.org), BabyCenter (community.babycenter.com), and The Compassionate Friends (compassionatefriends.org).

If your emotions scare you, don't be ashamed to admit that to someone. You've just lost a child. Give yourself grace and seek counsel. When we share our stories with God and with others our grief is lessened and our hope is increased.

· · · · · ● ● ● ● ● ● ● ● ● ● ● ● · · · · · · ·

Father,

Help me work through my rollercoaster of emotions so that I can find hope and healing. Please give me the courage to reach out and find a support group or trusted individual who will listen without judgment and provide encouragement and understanding. I trust You to bring the right support to me, Lord. In the meantime, I will be honest with You—my shield and my comfort—about my emotions and will pour my heart out to You daily.

Amen.

Day 4
Your Tears Are Precious to Him

"You have kept count of my tossings; put my tears in your bottle. Are they not in your book?"

—Psalm 56:8 ESV

* * * * *

THE IMAGE OF GOD CATCHING OUR TEARS IS OVERwhelming to me. I came across this verse shortly after our loss, and I could not fathom that the God of the universe held my tears. He sees our grief and does not disdain it. He enters into it. Because of this truth, we can give our grief over to Him.

He also longs for our honesty in grief. Your tears hold some honesty in them, but He wants to you speak it out loud from your heart. Several questions came with my tears. Filled with insecurities and hurts deep in my spirit that were far too complicated to express, I often just cried through tears, "Why God? Why take her? Why allow this? What is your purpose?"

Then I read the story of Gideon in Judges 6. Gideon was weak in His faith. He had experienced great conflict and defeat after being told by an angel of the Lord that He (the Lord) would save Israel and defeat the Midianites. I find comfort in Gideon's response. With honesty and frustration he asked, "If the LORD is with us, why then has all this happened to us?" (v. 13 ESV). I can certainly relate to that question. I've asked it myself more times than I can count. But, what the Lord taught me from this story in my grieving is that God didn't answer Gideon's "why." He simply responded with, "Go in this might of yours. . . . Do not I send you?" (v. 14). Sometimes, the answer is simply that God is with us and He is catching our tears. In your moments of tearful honesty, please know that He is with you, friend, and sometimes that's all we need to know. He meets us in our weaknesses and is accomplishing a purpose far greater that outweighs all of the tears we'll ever cry in this lifetime.

Lord,

Thank You that You are the Prince of Sorrows. You identify with my pain of losing a child because You sacrificed Your only Son willingly for me. Knowing that You are with me, catching my tears, is my hope for pressing forward. May I always be honest with You in my sadness, Lord. You are my safe place, and in You I know I'm OK.

Amen.

DAY 5
SOWING THROUGH TEARS

"Those who sow with tears will reap with songs of joy. Those who go out weeping, carrying seed to sow, will return with songs of joy, carrying sheaves with them."

—Psalm 126:5–6 NIV

*   *   *   *   *

I N YOUR LOSS, YOU MAY FIND YOURSELF LIVING BETWEEN a promise made and a promise fulfilled. The Israelites experienced this in their ascent to the promised land (Psalm 126). God promised them a land of plenty, but tearful sowing had to take place along the way. The crops were so bare, and as they scattered seed one by one, I wonder how many times they questioned where their next meal would come from? But they continued the work of sowing seeds regardless. For us, I think we can apply the same truth to our daily tasks in our season of grief.

John Piper offers an interesting commentary on Psalm 126:5–6 that I found so helpful in praying through our loss:

Sowing is simply the work that has to be done even when there are things in life that make us cry. The crops won't wait while we finish our grief or solve all our problems. If we are going to eat next winter we must get out in the field and sow the seed whether we are crying or not . . . So here's the lesson: When there are simple, straightforward jobs to be done, and you are full of sadness, and tears are flowing easily, go ahead and do the jobs with tears.

I'm grateful that our Lord is always faithful to give us the strength to persevere even when we don't feel like sowing anymore (Hebrews 4:16)!

Because of our sin nature, fear paralyzes and stops perseverance in its tracks. It doesn't move us through our journey toward hope any more quickly to hold on to our own plans and stomp our feet when we feel forgotten. He's not forgotten you, my friend.

After we lost our daughter in December 2011, not only did I have to push through emotional pain but physical pain as well. Because I waited too late in my laboring process to receive an epidural, it didn't take—twice. So after the tremendous heartache of having to say goodbye to our beautiful baby girl, I had to tackle the pain of fluid build-up in my spine. In visiting the emergency room to receive blood transfusions to my spine, I simply didn't want to sow. I just wanted to know when the harvest would come. I had to learn on the hard days, both emotionally and physically, to push through and sow the seed. Romans 5:3–5 became my life verse during this season of tearful sowing God had me in.

If you continue to walk through your loss, modeling Christ's response in pain, He will bring you out on the other side with hope born of suffering—a suffering that pales in comparison to what He endured for you and me on the Cross. So, if becoming more like Him is the end result, then keep sowing, my friend.

Lord,

Help me to continue sowing seeds even through tears. I know that Your ways are higher than my ways, and I trust You to fulfill the promises You've given me in your Word. I ask for Your strength and perseverance to work through me daily to help me find joy in the daily tasks. Even though my heart longs to find joy again, the demands of life make that difficult. Thank You for strengthening my heart to keep pursuing hope.

Amen.

DAY 6

WHAT IS LIFE LIKE FOR MY BABY IN HEAVEN?

"Yes, we are fully confident, and we would rather be away from these earthly bodies, for then we will be at home with the Lord."

—2 Corinthians 5:8 NLT

· · · · ·

I CAN RECALL WAKING UP THE MORNING AFTER ELLANIE died thinking, "What is my daughter doing now, Lord? What is life for her like with You? When I get to heaven, will she know who I am?" I became nearly obsessed with learning everything I could about heaven and what my baby girl's life is like there.

A resource that helped me greatly to understand what Scripture says is John MacArthur's *Safe in the Arms of God.* Here's what he has to say about what your baby's perfected life is in Heaven:

Your child will never have a selfish desire, never utter a useless word, never perform an unkind deed, never think a sinful thought . . . Your child will experience no suffering, no sorrow, no pain. Your child will never do anything displeasing to God. Because your child dwells in heaven where there is no taint of sin whatsoever, your child will live totally free of persecution, free of division, free of disunity, free of hate, free of quarrels or disagreements, free of disappointments. Your child will not weep because there will be nothing to make your child sad. Your child will know a life of unimaginable blessing—and only blessing—for all eternity.

How's that for overwhelming comfort? Whenever I read Psalm 16:11 I think about life for my daughter: "In your presence there is is fullness of joy; at your right hand are pleasures forevermore" (ESV). Whatever brings us pleasure and joy here on earth is multiplied beyond comprehension in heaven. And that's what your baby knows. That's all they know.

Because of the condition that killed our daughter—anencephaly—I love that she has perfect knowledge in heaven. Here, she had no brain, therefore she could not see, feel, hear, or move. In heaven she lives in perfect knowledge. She has more knowledge of God right now than I'll ever have in my lifetime! She lives free of confusion and ignorance. I can't even begin to explain the peace and comfort that brings. I know it may be difficult to imagine what your baby's life is like now because it's still painful to imagine his or her life apart from your own. But, I assure you that hope for restoration in your loss comes from understanding what awaits us all. The hope of heaven truly is indescribable hope!

Father,

How anxious I am to know the perfection my child lives in! I'm so grateful that my child knows undiluted joy and completion in you. When I'm caught up in my earthly emotions, remind my heart of the glorious hope of heaven. Thank You, Lord for the amazing free gift of salvation that is Your work alone! When I turn my eyes toward You and the hope of heaven, may the things of this world grow strangely dim, in the light of Your glory and grace.

Amen.

Day 7
It Is Perfect

"When the perfect comes, the partial will pass away."

—1 Corinthians 13:10 ESV

• • • • •

I MAINTAINED A DETAILED PREGNANCY JOURNAL WITH MY first child, Emmalyn. I'm not sure there's a mommy who doesn't. Ellanie was our second, and we found out we were expecting her when life was just a little insane. So I was not as diligent in journaling my pregnancy with her from the beginning. One of the few entries I did write, however, expresses my anxiety over routine and sleep and feeding schedules with a two-year-old in the mix. After finding those entries, I wished I could replace the anxiety I felt over those very small details with anticipated joy of having two precious, healthy girls to care for. Before learning of Ellanie's condition, God was accomplishing wonderful things in our lives. I even had friends tell me during that season that "things just seemed to be perfect."

Life may not go as we had planned,
but even still I am grateful that He is never
caught off guard.

After Ellanie was gone and the grieving process started to occur, the Lord showed me He is still perfect. For me to long for Ellanie to be here, experiencing life with us, is a normal human reaction, but it's not godly. Because what happened, in the way that it happened, is our Father's perfect plan. Everything He does is perfection because He is perfection. The perfection I am anxious to see in heaven one day is my daughter's reality now. It is all she will ever know, the reality she lives—whole and complete—forever. Proverbs 16:9 reminds me that while in my heart I may plan my course, the Lord determines my steps. Life may not go as we had planned, but even still I am grateful that He is never caught off guard. He knows everything that will befall us. We need Him to carry us when we can't take the next step, and that's what He is doing now, my friend. Some days, when the pain is too great, I can feel Him holding me in the palm of His mighty hand, and it is a feeling that I want you to experience as well (Psalm 63:7–8).

Sometimes, the only answer is that He is sovereign. One day, when we are joined with Him in the new heaven and new earth, we will have all the answers and we will know perfection. Until then, trust that He has power and dominion over all things and that His perfect plan is best. Even when you don't feel it, His Spirit is helping you to believe it.

Father,

When I start to think about what might have been, remind me that in You all things are perfect. Your ways are perfect and while I may not understand them, I do trust You. I want to experience You fully as the Author and Perfecter of my faith. When I start to blame myself or doubt the way things happened, bring me back to Your perfect character and hold me there. Jesus, You're my hope and stay.

Amen.

DAY 8
SCARS WILL FADE

"We don't have a priest who is out of touch with our reality. He's been through weakness and testing, experienced it all— all but the sin. So let's walk right up to him and get what he is so ready to give. Take the mercy, accept the help."

—Hebrews 4:15–16 *The Message*

I PROUDLY OWN A CESAREAN SECTION SCAR: ONE FROM MY oldest daughter, Emmalyn, and one from my son, Harrison. For the longest time, it was an ugly bright red scar, punctuated by red marks where the staples had been. Today, the skin is smoother and the staple marks are less prominent. But the scar is still there, a visible reminder of my childrens' lives—both of which have changed me forever. I have a different scar on my heart—one that will always remind me of the daughter I lost, which also changed me forever. And that scar is fading too. The weeks and months following Ellanie's death were the darkest emotionally and spiritually that I've ever known. For quite some time, I fought against anger, jealousy, and fear as I cried out to God for answers—answers that I wouldn't receive here on this earth, but that I would soon came to peace with. Over time, and through the tenderness of God's Word and the ability to share my story with other parents who were enduring loss, those scars began to fade. They began to heal.

Today, my emotions are more stable, my anger less easily kindled, the grief less intense, and the weeping less frequent. But the scars are still there. Invisible, they show themselves in moments that catch me off guard. Some of the moments

All of our scars, both physical and emotional, will be completely healed on that day, and all of our tears wiped away!

are beautiful cathedral-like moments and others, not so much. Nonetheless, I view them now as reminders of God's grace. That He is an ever present help in our time of need and that He bears scars because of us.

After Jesus rose from the grave, one of His disciples, Thomas, had trouble believing He was alive. He would not be convinced until He touched the scars in Jesus' hands—scars that John's Book of Revelation says will still be there when Jesus returns and will stay into eternity. All of our scars, both physical and emotional, will be completely healed on that day, and all of our tears wiped away! But Jesus' scar . . . it will remain forever. He sees your scar of loss, and He also sympathizes with it. One day, we too will be able to touch His scars and perhaps even speak the same words Thomas spoke: "My Lord and my God!" (John 20:28). Both of us scarred because of the brokenness of the world. We, a victim of that brokenness and He, the victor over it.

Lord,

May we never forget when we are reminded of our emotional and physical scars, that You also bear a scar. One that You willingly received for our freedom and out of Your great love for us. Thank You, Father, that you sympathize in our weakness and that You understand the pain we feel. Help us to find shelter in You and comfort in Your promise of life everlasting.

Amen.

DAY 9
COMPARISON IS A THIEF

"In peace I will lie down and sleep, for you alone, LORD, make me dwell in safety."

—Psalm 4:8 NIV

* * * * *

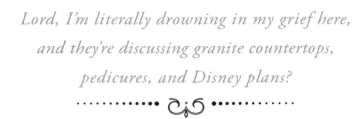

Lord, I'm literally drowning in my grief here,
and they're discussing granite countertops,
pedicures, and Disney plans?

IT SEEMED THAT FOLLOWING THE DISCOVERY OF OUR
daughter's birth defect, everyone was having babies, buy-
ing houses, and advancing in life. I know now that it may
have been just a handful of people in my circle of friends,
but it seemed like *everyone* at the time. And while I did my
best to express my genuine happiness for them all, it was
hard. The enemy is so quick to show us during our struggle
how wonderful everyone else's life is.

So, during our incredibly difficult season of tearful sowing in our lives and seeing no harvest, I decided to join a
ladies' bunco group. It seemed like the perfect fix at the time.
Life's hard. Play some bunco.

Everyone was discussing all sorts of great things from
kids who are seemingly perfect, to date nights, planned
Disney World vacations, and home-improvement projects.
While listening to them I couldn't help but think, *Lord, I'm*
literally drowning in my grief here, and they're discussing
granite countertops, pedicures, and Disney plans? It didn't
seem quite fair, and right then and there, I threw myself a
big, fat pity party.

I had tried to jump into a social gathering, hoping that the relationships would give me peace and make me feel safe, but the truth is I just found myself comparing my life to theirs and feeling more alone. I tried to hold on to the normal, everyday moments that I found myself pursuing before I lost my daughter. But all of the things I considered worth pursuing before became futile. I only dreamed of heaven.

May I encourage you not to compare your life to anyone else right now? It will only steal your joy, peace, and confidence and keep you from moving forward. Relationships are good, and surrounding yourself with others is good. But release control. You can't fix this on your own, and you can't be strong enough on your own. Stop striving to do like someone else, and just be. Lie down in peace, lay your head on His chest, and tell Him you're weary and that you want to see His blessing again. Seek His heart, even when you can't see His hand. While we feel like God may be holding out on us, He's offering what really matters. A more intimate, deeper relationship with Him. So while you think others may have everything that you don't, I'm challenging you to look beyond comparisons and think about the greatest joy even in the midst of your greatest heartache . . . Jesus. He is always better.

Lord,

I'm so glad that You see me, You understand me, and You know what I need. Please help me to keep my eyes on You and not on the lives of others and what they have. Hold me close and fill me with the peace that only You can. I need You now more than ever.

Amen.

Day 10

Where You Are and Where You Want to Be

"Woe to me that I dwell in Meshek, that I live among the tents of Kedar!"

—Psalm 120:5 NIV

• • • • •

· · · · ·

Six months before our daughter's death, the Lord had me studying the psalms of ascent. I had studied them before, so I was unsure why He took me back to them until I realized He was preparing me for the difficult path we'd soon walk. On the day I learned of my daughter's birth defect, I knew exactly why He'd given me those psalms to hide in my heart. I haven't forgotten them since, and they seem so applicable, even now. The promises of His truth are everlasting.

The psalms of ascent begin with a distress call. And I love the psalmist's honesty in it. I know I have had many of those moments, and there is no one better to express that distress with than my Savior. Even in the best seasons of life, it's still hard. In the pregnancy following my loss, my doctor ordered a long period of bed rest. She clearly saw without my disclosing my feelings that from a medical standpoint, where I was and where I wanted to be were two different places. So, she ordered me to do what we should do anyway in spiritual and physical crises—rest. I immediately thought of Psalm 120:5 and the pilgrimage of the psalmist. He was a long way from where he wished he'd be and not sure how he got there. He felt like a stranger in his own land.

Even among those who seek to destroy peace, we must press through our distress calls with humility and grace.

I still have days when my heart aches for heaven. Even though the Lord has graced us with precious gifts in our surviving children, I still miss Ellanie. I reflect every day on how her eternity is being spent and what she is experiencing there, wishing all the while that I could be with her. I'm reminded daily that as long as I'm here there will be endless distress calls. No matter where I may be living physically, I will always long to be somewhere other than here. I long to leave the areas of our daily environments that do not prioritize the gravity of the gospel and simply forget the conflict and trials that are, frankly, exhausting. Then I am reminded of the truth that He spoke so clearly through His Word after Ellanie passed that we are to continue living in and aiming for His peace. Even among those who seek to destroy peace, we must press through our distress calls with humility and grace.

Avoiding life here on earth is not the solution, but living in Christ is. If you find yourself in Meshek, living among the tents of Kedar, you must be honest about where you are until you can effectively journey to where you long to be.

Lord,

My heart yearns for heaven. I do not want to be here anymore, but I know that You have made it possible for me to live in Your perfect peace in the here and now. Help me, God, to push through the distress calls of life, understanding that this isn't all there is. My soul will wait silently for You alone, my expectation is from You.

Amen.

DAY 11
REFUSE TO LET GO

"Then he said, 'Let me go, for the day has broken.' But Jacob said, 'I will not let you go unless you bless me.'"

—Genesis 32:26 ESV

* * * * *

WHEN THE LORD STARTED SPEAKING TO MY HEART about writing this devotional, I wrestled with Him about it for quite some time. I promised myself when I clearly heard Him say, "go" I would, but for two years, there had not been that leading. I was refusing to let go of my story and give it over to God completely to use for His glory, when it isn't even my story at all. It's His. God reminded me about Jacob and his learning experience from wrestling with God and how he came out on the other side with blessing in Genesis 32:22–32.

I was reminded of some other instances in my life when I had wrestled with the Lord over certain things and came to realize that I've always considered wrestling with God a failure. I mean, who wants to get in a wrestling match with the Almighty, right? Surely, that's a losing battle. And then I started thinking about the term *wrestling* and decided that

The only way for you to lose in this journey to restoration and hope is to turn to your own solutions and devices, giving up the fight.

it wasn't necessarily a bad thing. In order to wrestle with someone, you have to be close to them. You can't wrestle with someone from far away.

So, instead of seeing my need to wrestle with God as a failure, I can choose to see it as intimacy—ultimately an act of surrender—refusing to let go of God and surrendering to His best for me. In this sense, wrestling means "surrendering and overcoming!" At that point of realization, I decided I'd keep holding on like Jacob did. Surely, if the Lord can use a man whose name means "deceiver," then He can use me. Jacob wrestled with God until God weakened him, but he didn't allow that weakness to deter him from insisting on a blessing. He held on to God. In the end, Jacob received a new name and the blessing he asked for.

The more I pondered it, the more the Lord opened my eyes to see that His desire was to show Jacob that Jacob's strength could not compare to the blessing He would give Jacob. He weakened Jacob to remind him, "You need Me more than you need the blessing." In that moment, I resolved to change my prayers to "God, I need ___, but not as much as I need you." The only way for you to lose in this journey to restoration and hope is to turn to your own solutions and devices, giving up the fight. It's a great mercy to be brought to the point where you are desperate enough to insist on what you need the most.

· · · · · · · ● ● ● ● · · · · · · ·

God,

If in wrestling You for a blessing through this season of loss, I come to know You more intimately, I will not let go of You. Like Jacob, I may limp for the rest of my life, but knowing You and surrendering to Your best for me is worth the struggle. Help me to desire You, Lord, more than I desire the blessing of healing or the blessing of another child. I need You more, Father.

Amen.

Day 12

For the Loved One Who Just Doesn't Know What to Say

"But encourage each other every day while it is 'today.' Help each other so none of you will become hardened."

—Hebrews 3:13 NCV

* * * * *

· · · · ·

W HEN I'M OVERWHELMED OR HURTING I WITHDRAW. I hide. I retreat. I am that friend you'll probably have to leave five voicemails for, ten emails, a couple of Facebook messages, and maybe even a pop-in visit. I loathe confrontation when I'm in a season of struggle; it's difficult for me to be around people.

I tried to send away relationships after we lost our daughter Ellanie, and it was enlightening to see, in the end, which friends stuck with me through my hardship and which ones got frustrated and left. Your loved one may need a push when they seem to just want to be left alone in their season of grief. For a time, they may think they're better off that way.

The Lord has reminded me in reflecting on our season of loss of the story of Naomi and Ruth. What a beautiful picture of strength walking alongside of crisis, refusing to let go and insisting upon encouragement. I love this translation of Ruth 1:16:

Stop pushing me away, insisting that I stop following you! Wherever you go, I will go. Wherever you live, I will live. Your people will be my people. Your God will be my God. (The Voice)

How could Naomi argue with that? She walked from that point on with a cherished friend beside her in her grief, bitterness, and season of struggle. Ruth stayed with Naomi even when she wasn't invited or encouraged to do so, and for Naomi it made all the difference! Just read Ruth 4:15–16.

God's plan all along was to bless and not to curse Naomi. He used that tenderhearted yet determined and pushy friend, Ruth, to bring blessing to someone whose heart was almost completely dried up and drowning. I have had friends be a Ruth for me in my season of grief, and my heart cannot adequately express the gratitude I have for their willingness not to give up on me. Our loss does not have to define our lives. It is not our lives; it's only part of our lives. The Lord can still establish in us an enthusiasm for what lies ahead.

To be a Ruth, you don't have to do much. A simple phone call, cup of coffee, time-out for a pedicure, call to prayer, or bringing a meal is more than enough. Ruths have come in and out of my life, and they have been an enormous blessing. Simply be there for your loved one, sharing in their grief and sorrow (Romans 12:15).

Lord,

Use me as a blessing in my loved one's life right now to bring the encouragement and support they need. Use me as a vessel of Your hope in helping to remind them they are not alone. Please give me boldness and courage to be strong in my own faith and to point them to Your love, grace, and mercy. When I do not know what to say, help me to turn to You. Be my tongue, my hands, my feet, so that my loved one may see You through me.

Amen.

DAY 13
GRANDPARENTS
ARE GRIEVING TOO

"Praise be to the God and Father of our Lord Jesus Christ, the Father of compassion and the God of all comfort, who comforts us in all our troubles, so that we can comfort those in any trouble with the comfort we ourselves receive from God."

—2 Corinthians 1:3–4 NIV

* * * * *

WE WERE LIVING WITH MY PARENTS WHEN OUR daughter died. We had just moved to Birmingham, Alabama, after living in Nashville, Tennessee, and then Daphne, Alabama. Both my husband and I were starting new jobs and getting our feet on the ground before deciding where we should live. When we received the news of our daughter's birth defect, everything just got put on hold. So, I intimately experienced my parents' grief as well as my own. I could see that their pain was on a different level because not only did they lose a grandchild, but also they had to watch their own child suffer in the process. Both circumstances were out of their control and realm of understanding. While my parents did everything they could to comfort, support, and encourage us, I could see that they, too, were hurting and needed encouragement. I know the mixture of emotions must be difficult for grandparents to balance—the innate desire to be strong for your child, while also wanting to crumble beside them in their pain.

While writing this devotional, I was able to witness the testimony of a grandmother who lost her grandchild just before Christmas. A fellow writer, she shared with me a letter she wrote her grandchild not long after she went to be with Jesus. With her permission, I'd like to share some of it with you here in hopes that another grandparent can find peace and hope in the ability to relate to her heart:

This precious little one will always be my first grandchild. I will think of her each morning as I fasten the chain around my neck that displays the November birthstone charm, every time I see a baby this Christmas, as I tearfully hold close the unfinished floor quilt that I was hand-stitching for Scarlett, and when I peer into the faces of my sweet and courageous daughter and son-in-law. My granddaughter's name is Scarlett Ray, and I have been forever touched by her.

—"Grandminny" Kim P. Davis

As God comforts you in your mourning, remember your loved ones are mourning too. Embrace the truth that He is near to the brokenhearted and saves those who are crushed in spirit.

Lord,

You truly are the God of all comfort. Your yoke is easy and Your burden is light. Help me to cast my anxieties on You, trusting that You will give me strength to help comfort and encourage others who are grieving with me. Give me Your eyes to see past my own suffering so that I can relate to the grief others are feeling in my loss. Use this experience to draw us all closer to You, Jesus. You are still good.

Amen.

Day 14
For You, Dad

"And I will ask the Father, and He will give you another Helper, to be with you forever."

—John 14:16 ESV

. . . . .

SOMETHING THAT WILL BE FOREVER ENGRAVED IN MY memory is the look on my husband's face when we learned that our daughter Ellanie would not know life with us. My husband is a big, brawny guy. But all 6 feet, 6 inches of him is tender and compassionate. Seeing him crumble at our news and do his best to comfort me while his heart was also tearing in two was difficult.

The Lord sees you, Dad. He knows your heart is aching alongside of Mommy's, and He sees that you want to make everything better for her.

I can see now that the Lord used our loss to bring us closer together in our marriage, but it is hard to convince one another of that in the face of grief. I do know that if there is one person in my life that I depended on more than the Lord to hold me up in prayer and encouragement, it was my husband. So, I'd like to give some words of encouragement to daddies reading this, who may feel useless or need confidence in their role.

Your wife needs you to depend on the Holy Spirit to pray for you when you do not know what to pray or to speak for you when you do not know what to say. As our helper and confidant, the Holy Spirit is groaning for you in this unspeakable loss. Tap into Him, and press hard into the discernment He gives.

The Lord sees you, Dad. He knows your heart is aching alongside of Mommy's, and He sees that you want to make everything better for her. But, you can't fix this. It's not a problem you can solve like a flat tire, and that's OK. Your wife doesn't need that from you. She just needs you. Your presence, your love, and your assurance that you still think she is amazing.

More importantly, she needs you to stay grounded in truth so that you can speak it back to her when she's weary and depressed. She needs you to put on the armor of Christ so that when someone unknowingly asks how the pregnancy is going, you can speak up for her with compassionate grace and integrity in God's strength. And on your bad days, when you're hurting and missing your baby, she needs you to tell her. Don't bury it. Let it surface so that she knows she isn't grieving alone. And if you seem to be advancing more quickly toward healing in your loss than she is, don't feel guilty. Its OK, and you can use that strength you're receiving in your healing to pour back into your wife. You are stronger in your journey toward hope together.

· · · · · · · · ● · ● · · · · · · · · · ·

Lord,

Please pour Your strength into me, that I may be an encouragement for my wife and family. Please open my heart to grieving as I should so that I can work through all of the emotions my wife is experiencing. I know that Your peace and grace is ultimately all my wife needs, Lord, but I also understand You have entrusted me with her heart to guard it and keep it safe. Help me to do so, knowing that Your Holy Spirit is guiding me and helping me along this journey.

Amen.

DAY 15
REMEMBER
HIS GOODNESS

"When my life was fainting away, I remembered the LORD, and my prayer came to you, into your holy temple."

—Jonah 2:7 ESV

. . . . .

• • • • •

THE STEPS OF THE GRIEVING PROCESS ARE DIFFICULT. But, I'm praying this step won't be too hard because it requires you to reflect on and remember God's goodness in your life. Even if in your mind your life hasn't seen much good lately, or ever, try your best to remember when you felt His peace, His faithfulness, His mercy, and His compassion. Remember who He has been and who He is, even in the midst of your terrible loss and sadness.

One of my little girl's favorite stories in the Bible is about Jonah and the whale. I wondered why she liked it so much, so one night when reading the Bible together, I asked her. Her response floored me. "I like it because even though Jonah did not mind God, God still let the fish spit him out." Such profound truth! Man, am I grateful that even when I turn from God to pursue my own way, He doesn't leave me in the pit (or the belly of a whale) to despair!

God placed a call on Jonah's life that he didn't care for. In fact, he flat out told God "no" and ran in the opposite direction of where God asked him to go. While my first instinct is to think, "Wow, Jonah, not very smart are we?" I have committed the same deliberate disobedience a million times without even realizing it. I tried to run when the Lord placed the call on my heart to minister to other women enduring infant loss. I was a children's minister at the time we lost our daughter. I was trying so hard to pour my heart into those efforts when God kept placing opportunities to write about our story in my lap. He also kept sending hurting women my way, even when I was still trying to heal from my own loss. While running from God didn't land me in the belly of a huge fish, it did land me in some pretty hard places.

What I love about Jonah is that he wasn't afraid to admit he was not OK with where God had placed him (Jonah 2:5–9). Instead he did something life-changing . . . He remembered who God is and all that is right about Him. You see, God hears our cries for help from the deep. He meets us in our hardest places of disappointment and hurt and lifts us out of it.

"Then the LORD ordered the fish to spit Jonah out onto the beach" (v. 10 NLT).

I understand if your loss is still raw and you do not feel like remembering anything good right now. It's okay to pour your heart out to the Lord and tell Him so. In that moment of grace and vulnerability, allow yourself to reflect on who God is. He is able. He is mighty. He rescues. He saves.

I encourage you to read the story of Jonah today (specifically 2:5–9) and pray what Jonah prayed if you do not know what to say. God will meet you where you are and encourage your heart. I promise!

· · · · · · · · · · ● · · · · · · · · · · · ·

Lord,

Like Jonah I have tried to run from You.
Your calling to carry this heavy loss is
hard. Some days, I feel like running in the
opposite direction instead of forging ahead
toward hope. But, I know that You have not
left me to despair. I know that Your way
is better, and while it may be hard, I am
confident that You will glorify Yourself in
it all. Help me to remember all that is right
about You today, God.

Amen.

DAY 16
KEEP YOUR
HEALING SACRED

"I am leaving you with a gift—peace of mind and heart. And the peace I give is a gift the world cannot give. So don't be troubled or afraid."

—John 14:27 NLT

Something I feel the Lord has charged me with as a wife and mom is to do my best to keep our home sacred. To embrace stillness. To let peace reign and for it to be a safe haven. When we lost our daughter Ellanie three years ago, we experienced that peace so closely, and I could quickly sense the Holy Spirit leading me to establish this for our home, wherever that was to be. I actually struggle more now to keep that peace consistent than I did through our loss. And I'm almost certain you will experience the same.

There are seasons for everything and this season now, of grief, struggle, and heartache is one to be cherished and kept sacred.

· · · · · · · · · · · · ♦ ᏊᏊ ♦ · · · · · · · · · · · ·

There are seasons for everything and this season now, of grief, struggle, and heartache is one to be cherished and kept sacred. It's so easy to turn our calendars into busyness and push our pain aside without thinking how it will effect the environment and people in your home. For me, it's difficult to dispense peace when I'm spread too thin. If I'm feeling pulled in twenty different directions by people or obligations on the calendar, it naturally affects the level of peace in our home and most importantly, in my heart. I find myself grasping to reclaim what I lose control of. I had to learn after our loss that it's OK not to be barraged by plans. Even the obligatory or "good" plans—do not let yourself become a slave to the busyness you've created to avoid healing. In creating no room for the sacred, we're allowing less margin in our lives for devotion to Christ.

In allowing godly women in my life to pour into me thoughts about protecting my joy during the season of grief, I realized that this obstacle to experiencing His peace was created by me. There's really not a quick, ten-step process. It takes time. Lots of sacred time. Safeguard your journey toward restoration and be intentional. "You will keep in perfect peace all who trust in you, all whose thoughts are fixed on you!" (Isaiah 26:3).

Father,

Thank You for granting me a peace that the world cannot give. As I try to find a way to integrate myself back into everyday life, help me to steady my pace and make room for sacred moments. I long for my journey toward restoration and hope to be filled with beautiful, peaceful, sacred moments with You. Fix my eyes on You, Lord.

Amen.

Day 17
Dance in the Rain

"I will send you rain in its season, and the ground will yield its crops and the trees their fruit."

—Leviticus 26:4 NIV

· · · · ·

· · · · ·

EVENTUALLY THE SKIES WILL OPEN UP AND THE SEEDS OF healing you're planting now will grow into something beautiful . . . something worth waiting for. In the meantime, instead of focusing on *why* you've experienced unexpected loss, I challenge you to prepare for the rain and expect blessing. Get your rain boots on and get ready to dance in it! Toil through your dry ground, expecting a harvest to come.

In the days after we said goodbye to our daughter, it was hard to imagine how the Lord would use our season of grief for anything good. The hurt, so fresh, and the tears, so plentiful, just seemed to dominate our every thought and breath. But three months after her death, we learned we were expecting our beautiful, healthy son, Harrison. Even with all of the fears and questions we had, little by little, day by day, God restored hope to our hearts and confirmed to us that He does "not cause pain without allowing something new to be born" (Isaiah 66:9 NCV). While that something new may not come in the form of a healthy baby, it may come in newness of healing and perspective.

You can still persevere in joy and hope
as you mourn your sweet child. He is worthy,
in spite of our drought!

· · · · · · · · · · · ৬ৡৎ · · · · · · · · · · · ·

You may be so deep in your grief that dancing sounds like the very last thing you want to do. Perhaps the drought has completely depleted any joy in your life at all. Perhaps there's nothing but sadness, turmoil, and mourning. I have been there.

May I just assure you today that in due season the rain is coming? Your pain is not in vain. Leviticus 26:4 (HCSB) says, "I will give you rain at the right time." Most translations read: "I will send you rain in due season." Verse 3 prefaces verse 4 with, "If you walk in My statutes and keep My commandments" (NASB). God makes this inviting promise on His precepts of obedience. And He has commanded us to be strong and courageous. We are to be diligent in our faith and dedicated to serving Him even as we grieve. So, what's the key to fighting this anxiety, sadness, turmoil, and fear in your drought? Exalting Christ through a life of obedience. Dancing because He's given us something to dance about, worshipping Him even when we feel like being silent. You can still persevere in joy and hope as you mourn your sweet child. He is worthy, in spite of our drought!

Father,

I'm so thankful for the rain that You bring and even for the drought that leaves me seeking You. Please help me to toil through my loss, digging ditches, gathering pails, expecting the rain to come. Restore hope to my soul so that I may display Your glory through this storm. May I never lose sight of Your desire to give me abundant life in You. Give me the strength to praise You through this journey, expecting blessings to rain down in Your timing.

Amen.

Day 18

Hope Born
From Affliction

*"My troubles turned out all for the best—
they forced me to learn from your textbook.
Truth from your mouth means more to me
than striking it rich in a gold mine."*

—Psalm 119:71–72 *The Message*

* * * * *

W E CAN NEVER KNOW WHAT HIS WORD MEANS UNTIL we are so afflicted that we cannot live without Him. Meaning must come forth from tragedy. Shortly after we lost our daughter, I found myself in the maternal emergency unit due to spinal fluid leakage. I remember lying there just three days after losing our baby girl and being released from the hospital thinking, "Please release me from this, Lord." Then, I heard a newborn baby cry as it was being carried to the nursery, and I just fell apart. I realized, the pain is not quite over, and the healing, learning, and reshaping had just begun.

Simply relieving us from the physical presence of grief is not what Christ died to bring us. He came that we might have life and have it more abundantly. As impossible and unreachable as this truth may seem to you right now, God can restore abundant life. He delights in mending broken hearts.

Jeremy and I have had several "proud parent moments" due to the impact that Ellanie has had in so many lives! Hope is born out of this. Our hope has produced more perseverance than we ever thought possible. So my prayer has been and will continue to be:

Father,

Please continue to bring me along so that I can rejoice in my sufferings because I know that suffering produces perseverance and perseverance, hope (Romans 5:3). You are the Creator and Sustainer of all things. Please transform my thorn into a flower. Help me to fully embrace the hope You bring.

Amen.

DAY 19

RELEASE YOURSELF FROM FEAR

"Do not fear, for I am with you; do not anxiously look about you, for I am your God. I will strengthen you, surely I will help you, surely I will uphold you with My righteous right hand."

—Isaiah 41:10 NASB

· · · · ·

IN THE WEEKS AND MONTHS AFTER WE LOST OUR DAUGHTER, I struggled to find rest. Both physically and mentally. My mind would race at night with questions that were mostly driven by fear of the unknown. It's OK for us to ask questions and normal for our minds to be busy with a wide range of thoughts during our season of grief, but it's not OK for fear of the unknown to paralyze us and stifle our journey toward restoration.

"And which of you by being anxious can add a single hour to his span of life?" (Matthew 6:27 ESV).

While my tears for Ellanie never ceased, my worry for the future eventually did when I allowed His peace and presence to wash over all my fears and fill every crevice in my soul. Eventually, I had to realize that I cannot control my life's circumstances by mentally fretting over them. You cannot allow the unknown to overtake your life and stop your journey toward restoration. When this happens, you must realize you have two choices: react to the fear that's making your mind, body, and spirit so restless, or turn to the Lord. When you react to fear, you're more likely to make irrational decisions that generally go against who God has called you to be. What we do out of fear never accomplishes God's purpose for our lives. I believe His purpose is for you to live in confident joy again, don't you?

Father,

Please help me to stop and choose You when fear starts to invade my mind and my heart. I want to live in peace with You, holding firmly to Your Word. Help me not to react in fear on my journey toward hope and restoration. I know that fear is just the enemy's way of trying to distract me from staying on this path. Help me to cling to Your truth that says You are with me and that You are strengthening me along the way. Thank You for the courage that Your presence gives, Lord!

Amen.

Day 20

A More Sensitive Mother's Day

"As a mother comforts her child, so I'll comfort you."

—Isaiah 66:13 *The Message*

* * * * *

THE YEAR MY ELLANIE DIED, THE SPRING HOLIDAYS JUST didn't bring with it the usual feelings of newness and hope. The first holiday was Easter, a day filled with hope and victory, and I only felt defeat. Then came Mother's Day, which followed what was my daughter's original due date. It was a painful reminder, and I often wondered if I'd ever be able to celebrate normally again. Since then, Mother's Day and I have developed an uneasy truce. I have two living, beautiful, healthy children who fill my days, my arms, and my heart, and I love celebrating with them. But I also remember what it felt like as I held my daughter in my arms and watched her slip away. And I remember what if felt like leaving the hospital empty handed, knowing I'd never know life with her here. And perhaps its survivor's guilt, but despite my many blessings, I found it hard to enjoy something I wanted Ellanie to have too. No matter what, you're always painfully aware of the gap between your living children and the souls who would have filled your home and your heart.

So, I want to offer you some suggestions for embracing Mother's Day in your journey toward hope after loss, and to help you welcome this day of celebration rather than wishing it away. Here are a few things that may make a difference.

Embrace the history of Mother's Day: Did you know that Mother's Day was begun by Anna Jarvis, an unmarried woman without children? A woman whose mother had recently passed away? This mother herself was a bereaved parent, with only four of her thirteen children surviving to adulthood. It was a day begun to honor the relationship between a mother and her children by a woman who had neither mother nor children to even celebrate. Talk about unselfish.

Embrace your identity: You will always be a mother. Death cannot steal that from you. If all of my children had died in my womb, during childbirth, after childbirth, in whatever way, I would still be a mother. Though it may not be obvious to the world, if the only children you have are with Christ in eternity, you are still a mother, and Mother's Day recognizes the relationship you will always have with your children. More than a mother, you are a child of the King. Your identity and your worth is not wrapped up in a holiday. It is wrapped up in the Cross.

Embrace your journey: Once upon a time, I had a plan for my life. Then one day when I looked back down the road I had traveled, it seemed very unfamiliar, nothing like the plan I had made. And of course, it wasn't. Because my plan was never the reality, except in my own mind. It was, is, and always will be God's plan, which is meant for good and not for harm (Jeremiah 29:11). As time unfolds, I have learned to trust Him and to be content with what He has given me and what He has not. His peace settles on my heart as I journey on toward hope.

You may not ever be completely comfortable with Mother's Day. But hopefully having a new perspective of its history, your identity, and your journey makes it easier to tolerate its yearly visit and perhaps even to welcome it in.

· · · · · · · · · ● · · · · · · · · · ·

Father,

I don't feel like celebrating Mother's Day,
but I know that the intent of its creation
was selfless, just as Your love is selfless.
Remind me that my identity is found in
You, not in being a mom. I trust Your plans
for me are to give me a hope and a future,
and I will rejoice this Mother's Day that my
child is with You—fully whole and fully
loved. Thank you, Lord for Your peace that
calms my heart on certain days when the
reminder of loss is greater than others.

Amen.

Day 21
Respond with Grace

"Gracious words are a honeycomb, sweet to the soul and healing to the bones."

—Proverbs 16:24 NIV

* * * * *

IF THERE'S ONE THING I LEARNED QUICKLY IN OUR experience of loss, it's that sometimes people just don't think before they speak. Or, if they do think, often it's not carefully or purposed with grace. I think it's because they feel such a need to say *something*, anything that will ease the awkwardness, yet their comments, when unfiltered, make things all the more painful. Like, "At least you know you can get pregnant." Or, "You're young, you can always try to have another." For me, because I already had a two-year-old daughter, I heard, "Be thankful for the child you have" a lot. As if having a child already rids your heart of the pain you feel from your loss. Let's just say I learned that I was going to have to prepare my tongue to respond to such comments with careful grace, so that the anger in my grief stayed intact.

It will help you to remember that your healing takes place when your speech and your response is draped with grace. If you allow someone's words to take the breath right out of you or pierce your heart, that only sets back your journey to restoration. Having a mind and a heart that's full of Jesus' love, acceptance, and perspective-changing truths will keep us from launching into a tailspin at someone's response to our loss. Make the choice, day by day, reaction by reaction, and moment by moment to consider grace without letting your emotions guide your responses.

"Let your speech always be with grace, as though seasoned with salt, so that you will know how you should respond to each person" (Colossians 4:6 NASB).

Lord,

You know the heart and intentions behind those who say what they say. Help me to respond to each person with grace, regardless of what they choose to say. Be my tongue and help me to control my emotions. Moment by moment I trust You, Lord. I am believing in You to season my speech with salt when the time comes.

Amen.

Day 22
Journey to Freedom

"In the day of prosperity be joyful, and in the day of adversity consider: God has made the one as well as the other, so that man may not find out anything that will be after him."

—Ecclesiastes 7:14 ESV

I KNOW WHAT IT TAKES TO BE FREE. I KNOW THAT IT IS accomplished in Christ because He's delivered us from sin and death! And I know that this changes everything. But there it is—in my journey through loss—are the ever-present struggles and hindrances that keep me from running with freedom toward hope . . . toward restoration.

When I was seven months pregnant with our son Harrison, I was put on bed rest because it was a high-risk pregnancy after having just lost our daughter. And as life would have it, this bed rest occurred during what was one of the most stressful seasons of our life. Yet, there was a steady peace calming me in it all. You could say I felt myself moving closer each day toward restoration because of the hope of Christ that sustains.

Standing in our kitchen, trying to handle needs with our rental home in Nashville and keep my blood pressure from rising in the process, my daughter came downstairs one day with that look in her eye . . . "Mommy, I don't feel good." Shortly thereafter—post vomit clean up—I had to call for reinforcement because I was chained to bed rest and felt helpless. Two days and a case of the flu for my daughter and a double ear infection for me later, I was asking myself what continually hindered me from embracing the freedom offered me? Why did I allow myself to be so easily discouraged?

For me, and most likely for you too, it always seems to be the unexpected inconvenient circumstances creeping their way into my life that serve as a hindrance. The unwanted weight that puts a wrinkle in my plans or throws my day off kilter. Can I say something to you? We have a choice. We can throw off the hindrances and choose to run through this journey in freedom—or we can surrender to the stress and anxiety the unexpected brings and live our journey in chains.

I love this quote from Beth Moore's *Breaking Free*:

God surpasses our dreams when we reach past our personal plans and agendas to grab the hand of Christ and walk the path He has chosen for us. He is obligated to keep us dissatisfied until we come to Him and His plan for complete satisfaction.

Jesus exemplified freedom all His life. He never allowed anyone or anything to hinder His accomplishing the will of God. He grabbed the hand of His father, and He ran. The Lord has taught me through the loss of our daughter to look for more of His grace in the unexpected and to embrace His hand when I feel like throwing in the flag.

The freedom given to us is hard to hold on to in the face of the unexpected. But don't let the unexpected threaten your journey toward hope and restoration! God's purpose in our temporary discomfort is not to hold us back or keep us from a better life but to strengthen and inspire us to run closer to freedom and the ultimate life—which is in Christ.

God,

Thank You for Your Son who sets us free. Free from struggle, free from sin, free from death. When the unexpected brings discouragement and loss of hope, please help me to focus on the Cross, which sets us free from anything we may experience in this life. Help me to embrace the power of the risen Christ that abides in me to run toward freedom in You. My heart longs to be fully restored from my pain to a fuller, freer life in You.

Amen.

DAY 23
OPEN YOUR EYES

"Open your mouth and taste, open your eyes and see—how good GOD is. Blessed are you who run to him. Worship GOD if you want the best; worship opens doors to all his goodness."

—Psalm 34:8–9 *The Message*

* * * * *

· · · · ·

ONE OF THE ENEMY'S FAVORITE THINGS TO WHISPER to me in my season of grief was that I couldn't be effective for God's kingdom. When I had my eyes fixed on my circumstances, it was easy to fall victim to that lie. But when I kept my eyes open, searching for teachable moments, focusing on Christ as my Source, it was a lot easier to ignore. What if we let God use our stories of loss to help encourage and teach someone else?

You aren't required to be OK with your loss to be used by God. He wants to take you just as you are and use you right where you are . . . tear-filled days and all.

I want to encourage you to taste and see His goodness and worship Him in it, even when you know you have a long way yet to go.

A few years ago, I was asked to speak to an infant loss support group. They had all experienced some form of infant loss and were going through bereavement counseling. I felt so ill-equipped to inspire their aching hearts when my own heart was still breaking over our loss in many ways. I accepted the invitation, but did not feel confident about it. I was looking to myself as a source of strength when I should have been looking to God. It was the first time I had told Ellanie's story in public, and I knew I'd be a mess. On the way there, the song "Lead Me to the Cross" by Hillsong came on the radio. In getting lost in praise and forgetting all about my anxieties, I heard the Holy Spirit so clearly. He said, "Maegan, even though you're not okay with where you are, you are covered. What Christ did for you on the Cross has covered all your broken places. You can go speak to these women not because of where you are, but because of who He is."

In that moment, I made up my mind not to let the enemy and his lies concerning my abilities determine my willingness to be a blessing for others, should God provide that opportunity.

Likewise, when I look at David's story, I am further sharpened. He wanted everyone to know what God had done for him each and every day. I think David was one of those who would talk to anyone willing to listen. It brought him such joy to share God's goodness, despite how bleak his life was! He was hiding in caves, fighting battles, and sitting around campfires with starving men. In the midst of it all, not only did he worship with eyes wide open, he led others to do the same!

Are you living with eyes wide open to see and share God's goodness in your season of grief and loss? I want to encourage you to taste and see His goodness and worship Him in it, even when you know you have a long way yet to go. It will help heal your hurting heart to open your eyes to others' hurts around you.

* * * * * * * * * * * * * *

Lord,

I know that You are fully able to use me in my weakness. Your strength is made perfect in my weakness. Help me to open my eyes to see Your goodness, even in my loss, and open my heart to sharing that goodness with others. I want Your glory to be displayed in my life and through my season of grief. Only by Your strength, Lord, can I be an encouragement to others.

Amen.

DAY 24
FUTURE GLORY

"For in this hope we are saved. But hope that is seen is no hope at all. Who hopes for what they already have? But if we hope for what we do not yet have, we wait for it patiently."

—Romans 8:24–25 NIV

· · · · ·

PAUL'S WORDS HAVE BROUGHT SO MUCH CLARITY AND comfort in our journey of infant loss. In reflecting on where he comes from and all that the Lord carried him through, I am certain that if anyone knew what real hope was, it was Paul. He knew what it meant to long for heaven, along with Job, King Solomon, and so many others throughout Scripture. I'm continually learning what "waiting" looks like and how it's an extension of our yearning for Him. The hope of heaven and future glory brings so much comfort and joy that I'm ashamed to say I've never yearned for it in this way until we lost our daughter. It is a deep longing that makes even a "good and full life" seem meaningless, apart from Him.

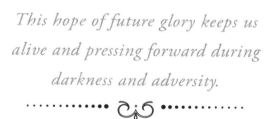

This hope of future glory keeps us alive and pressing forward during darkness and adversity.

When speaking to a dear friend about the indescribable feeling of being protected beneath the wing of God, she said something that reminded me how much I wish we lived without sin. She said, "This feeling will go away, so cherish it. Because we are naturally bent toward rebellion against God, this feeling will not always be there. The waging war against spirit and flesh goes on until we are with Him eternally."

In thinking about all of these things, I am so thankful that my daughter Ellanie never has to know what that daily battle looks like . . . the waging war of sin. She resides perfectly, without sin, nestled in our Savior's arms, and that makes me so happy. I have reflected numerous times on the words of Job. His pain and suffering was so deep that he actually prayed and wished he'd never been born. He said, "Why did I not die at birth, come out from the womb and expire?" (Job 3:11 ESV). He went on to say: "Why was I not hidden like a stillborn child, as infants who never saw the light? There the wicked cease from troubling, and there the weary are at rest" (vv. 16–17). Job was completely convinced that if he had died at birth, he would have known a better life than anything this life here on earth had to offer him.

How that makes me rejoice for my daughter! This hope of future glory keeps us alive and pressing forward during darkness and adversity. It is what allows us to experience even the tiniest bit of joy here on earth. Most of all, this hope of future glory increases our awareness of Him and turns our hearts toward things eternal. Like Paul, we wait eagerly for the redemption of our bodies and to raise our children in the new heaven and earth.

Lord,

Let my faith in future glory swallow doubt.
Thank You that my child has a better
existence than I do and that she (or he)
knows no pain. My child is worshipping
before God at this moment, and there's no
better place for her (or him) to be. Please
allow this truth to comfort my soul and
keep my eyes fixed on you. As I strive
toward hope in future glory, set my heart on
eternal things!

Amen.

DAY 25
THE GREATER REALITY

"The LORD defends those who suffer; he defends them in times of trouble. Those who know the LORD trust him, because he will not leave those who come to him."

—Psalm 9:9–10 NCV

*   *   *   *   *

· · · · ·

THE LOSS OF A CHILD IS A MOM'S WORST FEAR. HER WORST heartache. But do I love Jesus enough to say, "OK, Lord. Whatever Your will is for my child, I accept it. Both in living and in dying we will glorify you"? My husband and I lived the loss of a child once, and it was the hardest thing I have ever had to do. I find myself having to accept Jesus' will over and over again daily when I surrender plans for my children's lives unto Him and let go of my own plans.

I didn't know, before having children, the agony of giving birth to your heart and not being able to protect it. There is no comfort any human can offer in the loss of a child. But God is a greater reality than death. And losing a child *is* supposed to be heart-wrenching because otherwise God sacrificing His own Son wouldn't mean much. Our earthly pain is a mere tiny moment. Forever with God— and with my child who is at His throne right now—is my reality. *Forever* I get to spend with my child. Praise Him!

Paul Tripp says this in his book, *Forever:*

The belief that this present life is all I have makes suffering all the harder. You see, if present joy is all the joy I will ever have and someone takes it away from me, the impact is devastating. But if I know that this is not all there is, that God is moving me toward my final destination, then I know that this moment of pain is temporary. Living in light of eternity doesn't remove my pain, but it allows me to have hope in moments of pain.

When you get caught up in the present reality of your loss, remember that God is greater. Accept each day as God puts it before you as temporary; fulfill it. Then leave the rest up to Him. He's defeated death, and forever is waiting!

Lord,

I know You are greater than death. You
defeated death through Jesus' resurrection.
Because of this, I can place my confidence
in eternity and also in knowing You
understand my pain. While in this moment
my future feels defeated by death, I know
Your way is secure and through Your Son, I
have the hope of heaven. Help me to take
my eyes off this moment and place them on
You, my greater reality. My greater hope.

Amen.

Day 26
Jesus + Nothing = Everything

"More than that, I count all things to be loss in view of the surpassing value of knowing Christ Jesus my Lord, for whom I have suffered the loss of all things, and count them but rubbish so that I may gain Christ."

—Philippians 3:8 NASB

. . . . .

I FREQUENTLY SPEAK WITH WOMEN WHO'VE ENCOUNTERED infant loss. Whether through miscarriage, stillbirth, or birth defect, they've lost a gift that, to a woman longing for a child, is everything.

In writing this devotional, I've taken myself back to the moment in which I faced my own loss. My daughter Ellanie's original due date was April 24, 2012. While I try not to allow that day to carry any sadness, it still does. However, I'm in a place now where I can see that day for what it is—a date on the calendar that represents a thought of what might have been and a reflection of what is. And that God is *still* good in it.

Losing everything can indeed be the best thing for us. I am reminded of all the moments in my life in which God rewrote tragedy for His glory. If in losing your child you feel like you've lost everything, maybe you're right where God wants you to be. God is using this season of loss in your life for His purposes, dear one. And when we submit to His purposes, any death can be redeemed!

In grieving your precious baby, I know you must feel it's pain that you don't deserve and don't want. But it's ours. We can't send it back. But thanks be to our merciful God, no matter what happens to us in this world, something far better awaits us! Your child, risen in Christ, awaits. The Lord has taught me through my own loss that I really do not want this broken, sinful world to be the fulfillment of my wildest dreams. Give me heaven, please!

Father,

Please help me to see that even in losing
my child, I can still find everything in
You. Please use this season in my life to
fulfill a purpose that is greater than I could
comprehend or imagine. Use my child's life
to pen a story for Your glory. While certain
dates on a calendar may remind me of
what I do not have, help me to focus on all
You've given through Your Son.

Amen.

DAY 27
GRACE BRINGS CONTENTMENT

"We're in no hurry GOD. We're content to linger in the path sign-posted with your decisions. Who you are and what you've done are all we'll ever want."

—Isaiah 26:8 *The Message*

A SOURCE IS THAT THING FROM WHICH SOMETHING springs. How much do you truly depend on God as the source to your every need—including your desire to come through your journey of loss with hope?

When the journey of loss gets long, we may be tempted to search for other sources of comfort. It doesn't matter if your loss is fresh or if you've been grieving for years. In your weariness you may try to find substitutes for Jesus, but they all come up short. Hard days tempt us to put our security where God never intended it to be. It's a human response to reach out for what's tangible and what seems to bring peace.

I love that even Jesus, Son of the Almighty God, was willing to admit He was not the source of His own strength here on earth. He depended on His Father for everything and gave God the glory for the work He was given to do. Thankfully, God does not leave us suspended in a state of grief. He delivers us from our flesh and into the grasp of grace! And that wonderfully amazing grace brings contentment to our hearts (Romans 6:14).

This should be all the source we need in our pursuit to experiencing hope in our loss. Accepting whatever circumstance God allows is not weakness or settling for less. It is very much a part of a holy and obedient walk. And because we are united with Christ in all His power, He is our ultimate source of strength to walk through life without our child. Is He your source today?

Lord,

Be our source of comfort, strength, guidance . . . everything that's needed as we cling to You in our grief. While we do not understand Your ways, we do know fully that they are higher than ours. Help us to let go of our own strength and cling to You. Let Your grace overwhelm our hearts so that we can find contentment even in this hard place. You're enough, God.

Amen.

DAY 28
THANK HIM ANYWAY

"Devote yourselves to prayer, keeping alert in it with an attitude of thanksgiving.*"*

—Colossians 4:2 NASB, author's emphasis

I ABSOLUTELY, WHOLEHEARTEDLY BELIEVE THAT EVEN when living in a season of grief, we can still sow thankfulness. We can still live a lifestyle of communion with God and praise. That is, after all, what we were made for. What could be better than doing exactly what we were made for, regardless of our circumstance? Sometimes weariness can overcome our hearts. I know it has mine more times than I can count.

But even the unwanted is meant to be celebrated. Because in the unwanted, God's provision and peace still surround us. Gratitude for that constant provision and peace is the key to unlocking a joy-filled life, even after your baby is gone.

To find hope in our season of loss,
we must sacrifice our understanding of
what seems beneficial for us, lay down our
perspective, and thank Him anyway.

A life of authentic gratefulness is always thanking God for all things. In December 2011 we lost our daughter Ellanie due to a fatal birth defect. How could I thank Him for that, you ask? It wasn't that I thanked Him for the birth defect and the implications that it would have, but I did thank Him for the dependency it caused me to have on Him. In our season of struggle and suffering, I was able to see more clearly the simple blessings in my life I had begun to take for granted—for example, my steady, prayerful, and supportive husband Jeremy and my beautiful, healthy, and kindhearted daughter Emmalyn.

To find hope in our season of loss, we must sacrifice our understanding of what seems beneficial for us, lay down our perspective, and thank Him anyway. When dealing with the loss of a child, thankfulness can be hard. Nancy Leigh DeMoss says something so brutally truthful about a life of thankfulness in her book *Choosing Gratitude*:

Most of us are able to thank God for His grace, comfort, and sustaining power in trial, but we don't thank Him for the problem, just finding Him in it.

Like the rising of the sun, there is always something to thank Him for, even in the midst of the difficult, because we serve a God who never stops being good. Even though you're experiencing this indescribable loss, your life isn't meant to just be survived but to be savored. Will you savor Him today?

Father,

Help me to rejoice in all circumstances, even in the loss of my child. I know that You know what is best for me and what is best for my baby. Even in the unknown, I will give You thanks because Your faithfulness never changes. Open my heart and my hands to the simple blessings around me, that I may live a life of gratitude that glorifies You.

Amen.

DAY 29
WHEN YOUR HEART IS READY TO LONG FOR ANOTHER CHILD AGAIN

"Being confident of this, that He who began a good work in you will carry it on to completion until the day of Christ Jesus."

—Philippians 1:6 NIV

· · · · ·

I'VE RECITED THIS SCRIPTURE TO MYSELF COUNTLESS TIMES when my flesh told me to focus on what I did not have and what God had not completed. When you return home from the hospital empty-handed or from a routine doctor's appointment where you learned your baby has no heartbeat, that loss and grief are all you can think of. You will not have your heart's desire.

There will come a time, however, when you're ready to start thinking about having another child—or ready to open your hands to whatever else God has in store for you next. May I encourage you, as your heart moves to that place, not to put all your focus on the completed work?

I looked her in the eyes that day and told her that whether or not we receive the blessing we're holding out for, we've already received our happy ending in Christ.

In working with women, this is the one issue I deal with most. My husband and I weren't trying to conceive again after we lost our daughter. We had just resolved ourselves to be okay where God had us and were seeking healing. So, I can't image the difficulty of planning another pregnancy after loss. However, I do recall vividly all of the fears that came rushing back once I found out I was pregnant again.

Because this was considered a high-risk pregnancy, I underwent genetic counseling and testing, and I feared the same thing would happen to me again. I had to trust that the work the Lord began would be carried out to completion.

I remember meeting with an infant loss support group shortly after my son, Harrison, was born. There was a woman there who had been following my blog. She knew our story and apparently had been praying for a similar story for herself. She told me, "I just want a happy ending like yours. I want my healthy baby, and I want my happy ending." Tenderly, I looked her in the eyes that day and told her that whether or not we receive the blessing we're holding out for, we've already received our happy ending in Christ. It's heaven and it's the hope that one day we'll worship our Savior with our child—completely free and completely whole.

When you can walk in such complete trust and faith in the wisdom and love of God that you do not have to be living on the other side of the completed work . . . that's where He wants you. When we live our lives as if God has already answered our heart cries—with joy, confidence, assurance, and peace—then we are living in contrast to the world and shining so brightly the world must take notice.

· · · · · · · · · · ● · · · · · · · · · · ·

Lord,

I do long for another child, but I know
that Your timing and Your ways are perfect.
Please calm my spirit and help me to focus
on You and You alone, not the completed
work. Restore me to joy, confidence, and
peace so that I may glorify You in my
journey toward healing. I'm holding out for
Your blessing Lord, but most importantly
I'm holding on to You.

Amen.

DAY 30
It's OK—
Laugh and Live!

"A joyful heart is good medicine, but a broken spirit dries up the bones."

—Proverbs 17:22 NASB

· · · · ·

* * * * *

I CAN RECALL FEELING GUILTY AT TIMES WHEN I CAUGHT myself enjoying a moment or, heaven forbid, engaging in a bit of laughter. That mommy guilt never ends, does it? It took some time for me to want to do those things, but naturally the day came when something was truly funny and I laughed. And that's okay! I want you to know that the Lord wants to restore joy, goodness, blessing, and laughter to your heart. After all, He created laughter for us to be reminded that we are to live fully in this life enjoying Him and His blessings.

Psalm 2:4 (NIV) says, "The One enthroned in heaven laughs." He is the author of joy and He is OK with your laughter! It's a tension dissolver and an antidote for anxiety.

There are going to be some hard days for a long time, but enjoy the good time in each moment. Proverbs 31:25 (NIV) says, "She is clothed with strength and dignity; she can laugh at the days to come." It can be easy to lose our smiles in the midst of this hard journey of loss. You aren't alone. But remember that laughing is one of the best ways you can show those you love that you enjoy doing life with them. What a gift to leave our loved ones with memories of us laughing, even in the middle of our healing. Don't look up and feel like it was a lifetime since you last laughed. God has entrusted you with your life, your loved ones, your struggles, and your unique challenges because He has perfectly equipped you for it all. So don't lose your laughter. He has given us plenty of beautiful reasons to smile in our journey toward restoration with Him!

· · · · · · · · · ● · · · · · · · · ·

Father,

Please help me to find my joy in You.
Restore my broken spirit to find laughter
again. Help me to be in each moment and
see Your grace that's offered daily. I long
to enjoy my life with others, even in the
midst of my healing. Help me to realize
that laughter itself in many ways is healing.
Bring laughter into my relationships, Lord,
so that I may experience You, author of
joy unspeakable, in this journey to hope.
Thank You for loving me so much that You
want me to enjoy life, Lord.

Amen.

Your Journey to Restoration Continued

I understand that this is indeed a journey. And because healing is a process, there is something to be said for the little things along the way that provide comfort, peace, and closure. For me, writing provided those things.

I have always enjoyed journaling and blogging, but after my loss, it became so much more than a hobby. I wrote letters to my daughter, journal entries, and prayers to God. The letters to my daughter, specifically, were powerful because in those honest words written just for her, I learned things about myself and how I was processing my grief along the way. And I'm grateful that one day when my living children want to learn more, they can read those letters and know my heart. This section allows you the freedom to start this process if you wish. I want to leave you with a few tips and further explanation as to how writing can help you in your grief.

When we write, we give form to our thoughts and feelings. The brain undergoes an internal mapping process. This process of emotional resonance through words gives us understanding of our emotions. The act of writing gives form to grief and in doing so helps us move from being overwhelmed to learning to balance our emotions from day to day.

Writing about your emotions is good for your physical and emotional health. Research has found that writing promotes better health, sleep, immune system functioning, and a decrease in less healthy coping.

Writing can help create structure. When you've lost your child, things can seem chaotic and completely off balance. Writing involves intention, which can help provide some stability and structure.

TIPS:

- Make time to write. Set aside a little time each day—20 minutes or so—to process your emotions and train your mind to prepare your thoughts. You'll find the benefits of writing greater if you set aside at least 15–20 minutes to journal your thoughts, but do what you can. Even 5 minutes can be therapeutic. A few sheets of nice paper, a pen, and your favorite candle can set the right atmosphere for inspiration. Using computers, tablets, or other devices may help too.

- Acknowledge your emotions and write them down. Don't shy away from your emotions. Writing can help you process them in such a way that you're able to come to terms with the way you feel. Even if you never decide to make your writing available for others to read, it's still therapeutic to allow your heart and mind to process what you're feeling.

- Let your guard down. Let go of any feelings of blame or regret. The deeper the thoughts and emotions you write about, the greater the benefit to writing is. Explore the connection or lack of connection you had with your child. This can help you gain perspective on your feelings.

This is a letter I wrote to my daughter on December 26, 2011, just weeks after she went to heaven. Make your letter your own and just release your heart and soul to be honest with your child and mostly, with Christ.

My Dearest

ELLANIE BETH,

As I write your name, I'm reminded of the day Mommy knew we'd call you "Ellanie." I was sitting with your Gigi watching your big sister Emmalyn play when we started discussing baby names. You see, the next day we were to find out whether you were going to be a boy or girl and we were so thrilled and anxious. Mommy was a little nervous about the appointment because I was meeting with a brand new doctor in the middle of my pregnancy with you. Nonetheless, I couldn't stop thinking about names. I wanted to make sure I walked out of that doctor's office giving you a name. I had always had my heart set on "Harrison" for a boy, but was really struggling to find the right girl name. Mainly because I wanted to give you the same initials as your big sis: EBR. I had thought of "Ellanie" several times and really wanted to call you "Ella."

....

In mine and your Gigi's discussion, without her even knowing, your Gigi said, "You know an E name that I really love? Ellanie." I was shocked because I hadn't shared this to anyone at that point except your daddy. I told her, "I'm really drawn to Beth for a middle name. What do you think?" Your Gigi, whom you would have loved and adored, just as our Emmalyn does, looked as if she would cry. She said, "Maegan, I was just going to suggest that! I love it." Right then, I knew that's what we'd call you and that God surely had to have laid both those names on mine and your Gigi's heart for a reason.

....

Exactly one month ago today, your mommy and daddy learned that you were going to be extra special. Ellanie, I cannot describe to you how the love God had already placed in my heart for you instanta- neously and immensely grew. God gave me a strange sense of peace and strength that day. Although some say most of it was probably shock over our news, I am confident that it was the Lord preparing us for what we'd face. In the days to follow, Mommy just tried to cherish your sweet presence in my belly. I relished every kick (you were squirmy just like your big sister!), and I treasured every quiet moment, just you and me. Mommy loves old hymns, and because I knew I'd never get the opportunity to teach you about Jesus, I simply wanted you to hear of His great love through song before you met Him. It astounds me that right now, you have more knowledge of that unfathomable love than we do and that you're singing your own songs of praise in the fullness of His glory.

....

Your daddy was very strong too, trying to be a help to mommy and Emme, but I could see that his heart was breaking for you. You would have loved your daddy. I am convinced that because your sister is so girlie, you would have been the tomboy your daddy always wanted. Perhaps a little rougher around the edges, but still quite the "little lady" your sister is turning out to be. I know that you and Emme would have been best friends, as I am with your Aunt Lu and Aunt Nat. Ellanie, Emmalyn knows you by name and always will. We will never forget you, as you are forever a part of us. I assure you that your friendship with your sister will be the most perfect and complete relationship sisters can experience one day when she meets you in heaven.

....

Mommy is so thankful for the time we were allowed with you while God had you here, but my heart cannot help but rejoice with gladness that you are complete, whole, and perfect with your King! Mommy and Daddy would've always tried to protect you from evil, pain, danger, sorrow, and all of the terrible things that we live with here. But I admit that I am overwhelmingly grateful that you, Angel, will never weep because there is nothing to make you sad there. You will always know a life of unimaginable blessing and joy—for all eternity. Mommy and Daddy are also thankful, because of your condition, that you now live in perfect knowledge. Here, you lacked brain development, and there . . . you are a million times smarter than Mommy and Daddy put together! You will never know an unanswered question or confusing thought. You're living completely free of confusion and ignorance. We think on these things a lot when we start to feel sad about you not being here with us. We know and understand that you are fuller and happier there (Psalm 16:11).

....

That doesn't mean I don't wonder daily what life with you in our lives would be like. I knew the moment that I saw your sweet, perfect face and your tiny, flawless hands that you would have brought endless joy to us. I am so thankful that we got the chance to hold you as long as we wanted in the hospital. Those are memories that Mommy will hold onto forever. Your Aunt Lindsey said something to me in the beginning that I think back on often. She said that you were incredibly special for God to want you with Him so soon. Ellanie, you have touched so many hearts through your life. Mommy and Daddy have seen the Lord bring people back to Himself through our words about how God blessed us with you, Angel. That makes us the proudest parents in the entire world! No A–B honor roll, trophy, ribbon, or award could ever compare to that. So, when we start reflecting on all the things we will miss, we must remember that our precious baby girl's life story is having great impact for His kingdom!

....

So, until we see each other again, know that Mommy loves you and always will, my whole life. Sing pretty for Jesus . . . He deserves our highest praise!

All of my Heart *forever,*

Mommy

WorldCrafts^{SM} develops sustainable, fair-trade businesses among impoverished people around the world. Each WorldCrafts product represents lives changed by the opportunity to earn an income with dignity and to hear the offer of everlasting life.

Visit WorldCrafts.org to learn more about WorldCrafts artisans, hosting WorldCrafts parties and to shop!

WORLDCRAFTS℠
Committed. Holistic. Fair Trade.
WorldCrafts.org 1-800-968-7301

WorldCrafts is a division of WMU®.

New Hope® Publishers is a division of WMU®, an
international organization that challenges Christian believers
to understand and be radically involved in God's mission.
For more information about WMU, go to wmu.com.
More information about New Hope books
may be found at NewHopePublishers.com
New Hope books may be purchased at your local bookstore.

Please go to
NewHopePublishers.com

If you've been blessed by this book,
we would like to hear your story.
The publisher and author welcome your comments and
suggestions at: newhopereader@wmu.org.